text
Kathleen Bowman

design concept
Larry Soule

photos
Globe: pp. 6, 14, 20, 26
UPI: pp. 8, 18, 30, 32, 38
Minneapolis Star & Tribune: pp. 12, 36

published by
Creative Education,
Mankato, Minnesota

ON STAGE
JOHNNY CASH

Published by Creative Educational Society, Inc.,
123 South Broad Street, Mankato, Minnesota 56001
Copyright ® 1976 by Creative Educational Society, Inc. International
copyrights reserved in all countries.
Distributed by
Childrens Press, 1224 West Van Buren Street, Chicago, Illinois 60607

Library of Congress Numbers: 75-427-52   ISBN: 0-87191-486-7

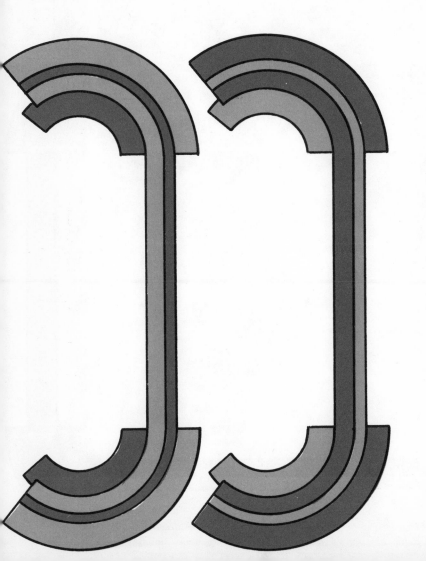

evening at the white house

In the East Room of the White House, President Richard Nixon leaned forward attentively in his chair, resting his head in his hands. He concentrated on a towering figure in a black frock coat and ruffled shirt, belting out songs in relentless baritone, swinging his guitar in time to the music. The man's name — Johnny Cash. Beside the singer was his wife, June Carter, whose throaty voice and bouncing steps seemed almost too spirited for the long white gown she wore.

Earlier in the day, Johnny and June Carter Cash had been brought to the White House in an official black limousine. Now on the gold-carpeted stage, flanked by Secret Service agents and photographers, they performed for 200 dignitaries.

President Nixon had never been interested in country music, but he had invited Johnny Cash to perform at the White House because of the

7

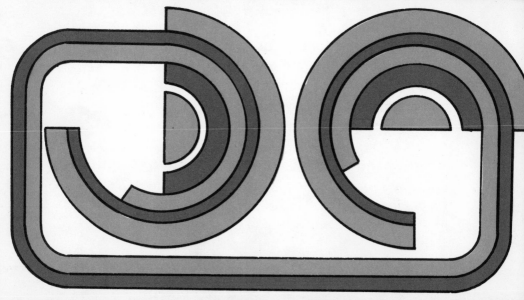

singer's support of the President's Vietnam policies. During the concert, with the audience so
caught up they were clapping their hands to the
music, Johnny Cash paused to repeat his backing
of President Nixon. Then he added, speaking
directly to the President who sat in front of him,
"We pray, Mr. President, that you can end this
war in Vietnam sooner than you hope or think it
can be done, and we hope and pray that our boys
will be back home and there will soon be peace
in our mountains and valleys."

There it was. Johnny Cash, a Martin guitar
slung around his neck and sweat running down
his face, speaking candidly to the President of
the United States. Johnny Cash — singer of songs
about cotton fields, hoboes, floods, and the Great
Depression; Johnny Cash — the champion of the
common man, with President Nixon and White
House dignitaries as his rapt audience.

And President Nixon listened. Perhaps because there were days in his own past when he'd
been an underdog, and he knew about the hard
times in Cash's songs. Nixon also knew that Cash
drew the respect of young and old, hippies and
hard-hats, rich and poor, hawks and doves.
Anyone who could unify these groups deserved
to be heard.

Later, as the guests toured the presidential
quarters, President Nixon told Cash, "It's the
hard knocks and the hard times that are making

you the man you are now. You're reaping the rewards of having realized the mistakes you've made and profiting from the hard times you've had."

Indeed, Johnny Cash has been reaping rewards and profits unheard of even in the world of superstars. He has recorded over 400 songs and sold 30 million records as well as over a million pre-recorded tapes. In addition, he has successfully starred in movies, performed on his own TV show, and composed songs for screenplays. Two corporations are needed to handle his business, which includes an income of over $3,000,000 a year. In 1969, Cash was named "Entertainer of the Year" at the Country Music Festival. That year he also received the awards for "Male Vocalist of the Year," "Best Album of

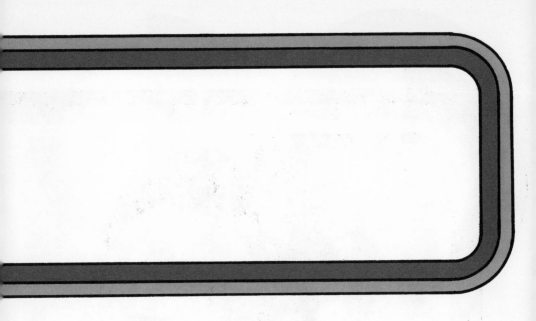

the Year," and "Vocal Group of the Year" (with his wife, June Carter).

Cash, who says he has adapted very well to prosperity, lives in a spectacular $250,000 house set into a limestone cliff in the Tennessee woods. Overlooking Old Hickory Lake, this elegant mansion with its nine-foot chandeliers and 30-foot ceilings reflects the astonishing success of the undisputed "King of Country Music."

But Johnny Cash's somber, weathered face reveals that his prosperity is the last chapter in a story containing periods of despair as well as triumph. His secret may indeed be that he learned to profit from hard times. For as his songs reveal, Johnny Cash reshapes his own experiences into blunt, convincing lyrics that call attention to what is common yet noble in the lives of everyone.

arkansas boyhood

Johnny Cash's origins are a stark contrast to his present life-style. He was born in a three-room railroad shack in Kingsland, Arkansas on February 26, 1932 — the fourth of seven children born to Carrie and Ray Cash. Ray was a poor dirt farmer eventually busted by the Depression. He hopped boxcars to look for work — picking cotton, chopping wood, driving cattle. Years later Johnny Cash would relate tales of his father's experiences in his songs.

In 1935, when John was almost 4 years old, the Cashes moved with their meager belongings to Dyess Colony in northeastern Arkansas. The government was offering a house, a mule, and a barn to anyone who could clear 20 acres of land. The Cash family made the 250-mile trip in a pick-up truck on wet, muddy roads in bitter cold. Young John spent the trip peering out the back window watching the rain freeze on the tar-paulin and icicles swing eerily from tree branches.

Dismal though the setting seemed, the Cashes stared admiringly at their new dwelling — House

No. 266. The $1,000 house totally surrounded by mud was better than any place they'd lived in. The children didn't seem to care that they had to sleep on the floor.

The entire family worked from sunup to sundown, dynamiting stumps and killing snakes so that the land could be plowed and cotton planted. But as these challenges were met and the rich Mississippi Delta land began to produce, nature posed another threat: floods. It rained for 21 days and nights that January of 1937, and terrified families watched water rise around them when the levee at Wilson, Arkansas, broke. The experience left its mark on 5-year-old John Cash, who in later life composed a song from his recollections. He once explained in a concert, "I woke up and that black, muddy Mississippi River water was right up to the front door, and I heard my daddy holler, 'How high is the water, Mama? Five feet high and rising'."

Music became a vital way for the Cash family to ease tensions and remain spiritually intact despite hardship. They often sang traditional Baptist hymns in the cotton fields and around the old upright piano Carrie had bought for $37.00. One of Johnny Cash's hit songs, "Daddy Sang Bass," was to recall these moments: "Just poor people that's all we were/Tryin' to make a livin' out of black land dirt; We'd get together in a fam'ly circle singin' loud."

15

Of all the Cash children, Johnny was most captivated by music. He sat alone for hours with his ear against the huge battery-powered radio, absorbed in country and western music. Soon he was singing along with the Carter Family, Jimmie Rodgers, and Red Foley. Carrie once recalled that he was so preoccupied that "even when I'd ask him something a second time, his mind would seem to be far away. I guess he was really taken by those tunes and maybe he was thinking of the things he'd do someday. . . ."

Carrie Cash encouraged her son's interest in music by taking in washing and ironing to get the fifty-cents for Johnny's first singing lesson. After one month his teacher told Johnny not to change the way he sang. She also confessed to Carrie that Johnny's voice was so unique there wasn't much to teach him.

John's growing attraction to music and to the world it represented often interfered with his work. At 14, Johnny got a job hauling water from farms to the crews digging railroad banks along the Tyronza River. But the workers' parked cars were too great a temptation. As he passed them with his water buckets, he'd slip inside, turn on the radio and listen to country music. At the end of the day, angry, thirsty men returned to their cars to find the batteries mysteriously dead.

It was the country singers Johnny Cash heard on the radio who started him dreaming of a life beyond the farms and poverty of Dyess. For the restless, solitary youth the fantasies were later to become reality. But he has never lost touch with his early days on the cotton farm. Echoing President Nixon's words, Johnny Cash has said, "If I hadn't grown up there, I wouldn't be what I am now. It was the foundation for what I became."

Like most youth in Dyess, Johnny left the farm in search of steady wages. After graduating from high school, he took a bus to Detroit and got a job on a punch press in the Fisher body plant. He lasted only two weeks, then hitch-hiked back to Dyess, lonely and discouraged. He has said, "Detroit was like a foreign country to me. I never had been more than 50 miles away from home. . ."

The only work available on the farm, now rented out, was light chores, so Johnny did odd jobs at a nearby factory where his father was foreman. Again, restless and disillusioned, he quit after two weeks. Then one summer day in 1950, unable to find work that satisfied him, he enlisted in the Air Force.

"The Air Force was where I started finding myself," Cash says now. "I was proud of the work I was doing, because I excelled in it." With a determination and involvement lacking in earlier jobs, Johnny completed a challenging training period for radio intercept operators.

He transcribed Morse code so rapidly he was chosen to monitor international flight traffic in Landsberg, Germany. Happily for Cash, several other country music buffs lived with him in the Landsberg barracks, and they taught Johnny his first chords on a $5 German guitar. Eventually, Johnny and his buddies formed a group called the "Landsberg Barbarians." They lived up to their name by bursting into German taverns singing country tunes to guitar and mandolin.

Johnny worked rigorous eight-hour shifts, sitting with earphones on recording Soviet radio traffic. Because of his keen hearing, he was given increasingly difficult assignments.

The tension of the job mounted, but Johnny was a loner who kept his feelings to himself. Suddenly one night he picked up his typewriter and hurled it through the window, bursting into tears. Johnny was wrestling with a combination of isolation, stress, and violence that was to plague him later in life.

Although Johnny was a staff sergeant at the end of his four years, he chose not to re-enlist. But the Air Force experience had given him a chance to play and sing country music, and by the time of his discharge he was not only performing, but composing songs as well. He had developed enough confidence to try making a living at music.

on the air

"I got the idea that I might break in through the back door," Johnny has said. "I decided to take a radio-announcing course that would get me a job as a disc-jockey, which in turn might open a way into one of the studios."

So it was that Johnny Cash, just married to Vivian Liberto and living in Memphis, began his career in music. But he also took a job as a salesman for an appliance company to support Vivian and himself.

Cash's dismal history of employment repeated itself. The quiet, solitary musician was no salesman. "I hated trying to convince people they should have something they didn't really want. I felt dishonest."

When Johnny was making door-to-door sales, if he saw a guitar in a home he'd sit down and play, completely forgetting his company's washing machines. Music's ability to lure the restless Cash away from jobs could easily have inspired the lyrics for "Tennessee Flat Top Box," which he later wrote, "Well, he couldn't drive a wrangle/And He never cared to make a dime;/But give him his guitar/And he'd be happy all the time."

One day Johnny's brother Roy, a service manager at a garage, took him over to the shop to meet two mechanics, Marshall Grant and Luther Perkins. It was a significant meeting, for both Marshall and Luther played guitar and were eventually to become Johnny's sidemen. "Before I ever shook his hand," Grant later said, "before I ever spoke to him, I saw him coming down the rows of cars, and he seemed almost magnetic . . . there was something that caught your attention. He was tall and dark, and he was as edgy as a cat on a hot tin roof . . ."

Soon the three musicians were playing together nightly in each other's homes. One time Johnny suggested that they try instruments besides acoustical guitars. So Luther borrowed an electric guitar and Marshall got hold of a bass — an instrument he'd never played.

None of them could read a note of music, as is often true of country musicians. But they taught themselves to play with long hours of practicing together. As the group became more confident they performed their songs at church barbecues and benefits.

Johnny was still making a meager $20 a week selling appliances. He held his job only because his boss, George Bates, had taken a liking to him. One day Bates asked Johnny what he really wanted to do. Johnny said he'd like to sing on the radio and someday make a record. Bates offered to sponsor the group on a radio show. So for eight Saturday afternoons the trio played 15 minutes of gospel music on country station KWEM.

That experience was enough to convince Johnny to try to make a record. The group decided to go to Sun Records in Memphis, which had just recorded Elvis Presley.

Director Sam Phillips agreed to the audition, but after hearing them play, he told them there was no market for gospel music. The new trend was rock 'n roll. Cash said he had a song like that — one he'd written in the Air Force. He ran through "Hey Porter." Sam Phillips approved and told Cash that if he could come up with one as good for the flip side, he'd do the record.

Elated, Johnny went home and wrote "Cry, Cry, Cry." While waiting to audition again, the group began experimenting. John put a piece of paper between the guitar strings and the frets, creating a sound like brushes on a snare drum. Luther learned to hit a note, muffle the strings with the heel of his hand, and hit the note again, creating the **boom-chucka-boom** that has since characterized Johnny Cash's songs. Marshall Grant's contribution to the new sound was a $44.65 electric amplifier.

The evening of the second audition, Sam Phillips recorded "Hey Porter" after only four takes. The flip side took much longer. Cash recalled, "We must have tried it 35 times. Poor Luther just couldn't play it. He was trying to play the melody, and I showed him a break using runs on the guitar. . . ." After a long night, the group had cut its first record.

The next day Phillips wanted to know what they would call themselves. Cash suggested "The Tennessee Three," but Marshall objected since Cash would be doing all the singing. Grant thought it should be "John Cash and the Tennessee Two." Phillips said "**Johnny** Cash and the Tennessee Two" would have more appeal to the growing teenage market, so that name was agreed upon.

Johnny Cash signed the Sun contract. The Arkansas farm boy-turned-musician had never read legal language, so when he read "for one dollar and other considerations" in the contract, he stood around for an hour waiting to be paid. Finally, he left with 15¢ in his pocket. "It wasn't enough for a pack of cigarettes, so when this

panhandler stuck his hand out, I gave it to him."

As months passed, Cash began to wonder if the record would ever be released. But one morning as Marshall Grant drove to work with the radio on, he heard the disc jockey announce "Cry, Cry, Cry." When the song was over, the disc jockey commented, "I don't know these boys, but I've never heard anything come in with such a different sound. It won't be the last you hear of them."

How right he was. The record sold over 100,000 copies, eventually becoming number 14 in the nation. For Marshall Grant and Luther Perkins, whose only goal had been to hear themselves on the radio, the success of the record was a bewildering surprise. But for Johnny Cash, who had been dreaming of a career in country music since his lonely days on the cotton farm, it was only the start of a fantasy becoming reality.

on tour

"I decided after a few show dates," Johnny recalls, "I was gonna try to make a living singing and playing shows. So I got in my Plymouth and drove all over northeastern Arkansas, dropping in at theatres and schoolhouses, asking them if I could book myself in there to play a show." In the late 1950s Johnny and the Tennessee Two began playing intermissions, high schools, and ball parks, making barely enough to pay for the gas. The microphones were bad and the lighting dim, but it was in such settings that Johnny Cash began to sense his power over an audience and the loyalty the people returned.

Eventually Johnny toured with Elvis Presley and sang on the "Louisiana Hayride" with audiences in the thousands. These appearances and the one-night stops kept the group alive. Although the driving and the schedule were torturous, Johnny was able to compose more songs. He'd scribble a few words and a guitar run or two on a piece of paper, tuck it into his pocket, and sometime later dig it out and work on it again. Cash still works this way, though he's traded the scraps of paper for large yellow legal pads in a black folder. "The ideas come in little bits or big pieces," he says. "I write them down

27

and sometimes I carry them around for years, in my head."

The group's first nationwide hit, "I Walk the Line," was composed in this manner. While he was in the Air Force, some of Johnny's buddies had borrowed his tape recorder to experiment with their guitars. They accidentally rewound the tape backwards so that later when Johnny came back and turned on his recorder, he heard a strange, unidentifiable melody. It haunted him, and he began practicing the guitar runs he heard, following each one with the now-famous words, "Because you're mine, I walk the line." Years later in Longview, Texas, the rest of the song suddenly came to him. The recorded song became the nation's number one seller in popular as well as country music.

With the success of this record, music became serious business for the trio. Luther Perkins and Marshall Grant left their mechanics' jobs, and the group took on a manager — Bob Neal. Neal capitalized on what Marshall Grant first observed about Cash — his size, his magnetism, his complexity. There would be no sequined shirts and cowboy hats for a singer of Johnny Cash's stature. Rather, he would be a towering figure in black — frock coat, pants, and patent leather boots, suggesting simultaneously something of the gunfighter, frontiersman, and

preacher.

It worked. Crowds went wild in Philadelphia, New York, Los Angeles, and Detroit — cities where ordinary country music wouldn't have succeeded at that time. Radio and TV appearances drew millions of fan letters. And several companies fought for recording dates. Johnny Cash, the ex-farm boy, had suddenly become the most sought-after, talked-about musician in the country.

But success began to take its toll. Cash was on the road eight months out of the year. His life became a blur of hotel and motel rooms, crumpled clothes, and schedules — a dismal counterpoint to the bright lights and applause of the performances. To relieve the monotony, the group began to amuse themselves with practical jokes. They started innocently setting off firecrackers at the side of the road but became more destructive as oneupsmanship took hold.

Eventually the vandalism gave other country musicians a bad name. Hotels refused to rent rooms to them. But a more serious aspect of the problem was what the violence said about Johnny Cash. He was becoming destructive just as he had reached the heights of success.

Next, Cash's destructiveness turned against himself. He began taking rapidly increasing amounts of amphetamines or "pep pills." At first he took the pills to give him confidence for his performances. As Johnny became more popular,

his schedule became more hectic. By 1961 he found himself travelling 300,000 miles a year to give 290 shows. Then fatigue forced him to use the pills to stay awake. When performances were over, he'd need tranquilizers to get to sleep. Soon Cash was caught in a cycle of "uppers" and "downers."

For the next seven years, Johnny Cash continued to increase his drug consumption until he was taking over 100 pills a day. He became moody, lost weight, and developed voice problems. Just when he had risen to new heights of fame and financial security, Johnny Cash seemed to be in a downward spiral. Looking back to those days he has said, "Maybe I was afraid to face reality then. I wasn't very happy then. Maybe I was trying to find a spiritual satisfaction in drugs."

The roots of Johnny's unhappiness were many. The strain of performing was complicated by a failing marriage. The primary factor in his unhappiness, according to some observers, was Cash's inability to adjust to his sudden success in a rich and foreign world. If success was uncomfortable, perhaps Johnny Cash was trying to destroy it.

digging out

One person was determined not to let Johnny ruin himself or his hard-earned success. That person was June Carter. She had been singing with the group since 1961. June was a member of the famous Carter Family Johnny had once listened to over his radio back on the farm. Perhaps it was this childhood connection that allowed June to penetrate Johnny's isolation as no one else could. She relentlessly confronted him about his habit. "You're a better man than that," she announced after flushing his pills down the toilet, "and you're not going on stage that way."

With Marshall Grant's help, June kept the drugpushers away, searched out hidden pills, and covered for Johnny when he wandered in late for a show. And because the amphetamines destroyed his appetite, she would tempt him with ham and egg sandwiches or homemade biscuits that she made on the grill in the van.

Many times, June thought she had lost the battle. Following a concert in October of 1965, Johnny Cash disappeared. Two days later, a Nashville radio station called June with the news that Johnny had been arrested in El Paso for bringing drugs across the border from Mexico. He spent the night in jail, and although his sentence was suspended, the arrest was jolting enough to keep him off pills for month.

But the Musicians' Union had threatened to bar him, and his wife Vivian filed for divorce. His depression deepened until he was taking more pills than ever.

A turning point came in 1967, after Johnny Cash purchased the land he now lives on and moved into the house while it was still under construction. Needing a refuge, he spent long, solitary hours in the woods, hunting and fishing. One chilly morning Braxton Dixon, the builder of the house who had become Johnny's good friend, stopped by to see him. His car was there, but Johnny was not to be found. Suddenly Braxton saw Cash's tractor down in the lake — underwater.

He tore down the hill, expecting Johnny to be pinned and drowned beneath the machine. Then he noticed Cash clutching a tree, with his wet leather coat frozen stiff. Having jumped clear of the tractor as it hit the water, Johnny was too weak from drugs to climb back up to the house. In another half-hour Johnny Cash would have frozen to death.

When June arrived at the house she told Johnny she was giving up. Johnny begged her to call Dr. Nat Winston, the banjo-playing psychiatrist he had earlier rejected. With June at his side,

Cash vowed to Winston that he needed help and was going off pills forever. Nat Winston agreed to help, though he estimated the chances at three million to one that Johnny could shake the habit.

"If he's going to make it," Winston declared, "He needs friends around him." So for ten days, the doctor and Cash's close friends watched as June gave Johnny fewer and fewer pills. Quitting the pep pills took only two days, but the tranquilizers were more difficult. Johnny suffered terrible withdrawal pains and hideous nightmares. It was the most frightening experience of his life. But as his dependence decreased, he began to run regularly through the woods, and his appetite returned.

Cash went back on the road only three weeks after going off pills. He still wrestled with the craving for drugs and occasionally hid some away. But eventually he stopped altogether. Nat Winston commented, "Relapses are possible, but I don't think he'll ever have trouble again. I wouldn't make that statement about anybody else I know who has ever been on drugs."

Cash's return to music was spectacular. He soon found himself playing at Carnegie Hall and the London Palladium, where the crowds were larger than those assembled to hear the Beatles. As his career mushroomed, he did a successful television show on prime time, sold millions of

additional records, and starred in Hollywood films. A documentary based on his own life for educational television was so well-received that it was made into a full-length feature film.

By then his life included June Carter as both co-performer and wife. Three weeks after they received the 1969 Grammy Award for their famous duet, "Jackson," June Carter and Johnny Cash were married in a private ceremony in Kentucky. To this day, both of them deny that it was June who got Johnny off drugs, even though she was a powerful influence. "It wasn't even happiness with June that made me do it," Cash has said. "It was **me** that made me do it."

Many people on Music Row in Nashville were startled by Cash's comeback. After all, two singers before him, Jimmie Rodgers and Hank Williams, had met with tragic deaths. Johnny has said, "Oh, yeah, they all acted like they were proud for me when I straightened up. Some of them are still mad about it though. I didn't go ahead and die so they'd have a legend to sing about and put me in hillbilly heaven!"

compassion

The poverty of his youth and the lonely hardships of his early career have given Johnny Cash special insight into many of society's oppressed people. Even though he shuns the role of crusader, his songs vividly portray the plight of American Indians and prisoners.

One-quarter Cherokee himself, Johnny Cash protested the treatment of American Indians long before it became a popular cause among entertainers. As early as 1957, Cash wrote a protest ballad, "Old Apache Squaw," in Tucson, Arizona. Later Cash devoted an entire LP album, **Bitter Tears,** to describing the plight of American Indians.

One of the songs, "The Ballad of Ira Hayes," created a stir. It tells the true story of a young Pima Indian Marine who raised the flag on Iwo Jima in the midst of heavy fighting in World War II. Years later, Ira Hayes died drunk and alone in a ditch — rejected by the land he tried to save.

Afraid of controversy, disc jockeys refused to play the song; an editor of a country music magazine demanded Cash's resignation from the Country Music Association, accusing the singer of being "just too intelligent to associate with plain country folks, country artists, and country

DJs." Johnny Cash countered by saying they were afraid of the truth and sang the song louder than ever.

Cash does more for the American Indians than just sing about them. In May, 1970, when National Educational Television produced the film **Trail of Tears,** Cash starred as John Ross, the chief of the Cherokee nation. The film recounts the true story of Cherokees being driven from their homes to an Oklahoma reservation in 1838.

Cash also sings without charge at Indian benefits. Once he turned down a $10,000 television appearance in England to perform on a reservation in South Dakota. He also helped the Senecas protest the damming of the Allegheny River; perhaps his own boyhood on the farm helped him understand the Seneca's fears that the waters would flood their ancient burial grounds.

Johnny Cash is most widely known, perhaps, for his compassion for prisoners. "I don't see anything good come out of a prison," he argues. "You put them in like animals and tear the souls and guts out of them and let them out worse than when they went in." Johnny began singing in prisons long before he spent a night in jail. He has said many times that prisoners are the best audiences he plays for.

In January, 1968, after five years of argument,

Johnny Cash finally persuaded Columbia Records to record a prison appearance live. The resulting album, **Johnny Cash at Folsom Prison,** sold almost two and a half million copies and won a Grammy Award. When he sings "Folsom Prison Blues," Johnny asks the listeners to "hear the sounds of the men, the convicts — all brothers of mine." The LP also records clanging prison doors, public address systems and the wail of sirens — all testimony to the dismal life inside the walls.

At San Quentin, Cash's protest against the inhumanity of prisons was even more blunt as he sang, "San Quentin, may you rot and burn in Hell." The prisoners stood on tables and shouted him on. So did the public. **Johnny Cash at San Quentin** outsold the Folsom LP and was voted Country Music Association's album of the year.

But the rewards for Cash are more than record sales. After a show at Leavenworth, a convict wrote Johnny on prison stationery:

During the few hours you were here, I was no longer doing life in prison . . . It's a good thing the warden didn't do a head count during your show, Johnny, because you took us all out of prison and allowed us that much escape to freedom and the things we love.

The convict's letter says a great deal about the nature of Johnny Cash's wide appeal. Many

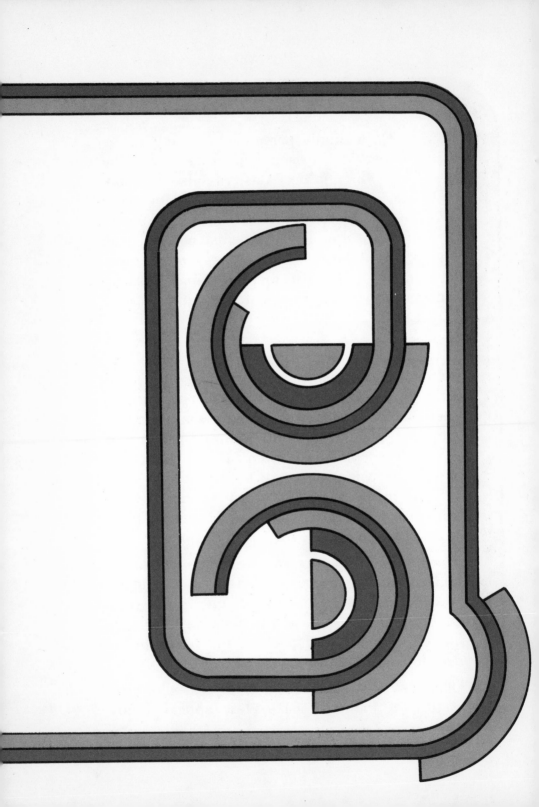

people often feel that life is a prison. His songs speak directly to everyone's loneliness and feelings of separation from others. Listening to Johnny's music allows people to "escape to . . . the things we love.'

Cash's stances on issues tend to be as complex as his personality. Refusing to be categorized on the issues of the Vietnam War, he called himself, a "dove with claws." He has said, "The only good thing to come out of a war is a song," but he stood behind President Nixon's Vietnam policies. Yet when it came time to select guests for his first television show, he fought with network executives to have Pete Seeger (a well known anti-war protestor) on the list.

His annoyance with those who put labels on him is expressed in the following statement: "Don't ask me what I think about anything unless you want to know about the next five minutes. My mind changes all the time . . . I'm changing, I'm growing, I'm becoming."

"Public life is unbelievable," Johnny Cash has observed. "If your face is familiar you are stared at, pointed at, laughed at, whispered at, yelled at, and followed."

Success for Johnny Cash has meant paying a price as well as reaping rewards. He often expresses sadness over his loss of privacy, especially in his home. A security guard sits outside his room all night long, and on weekends a policeman is on duty to keep sightseers from crawling over fences with their cameras and peering in windows. But he says of his fans, "They're great people, even if they do come out to your house by the busload."

What troubles him most is the power his fame and appeal have given him: "Twenty state governors called me in the last year to get favors from me . . . I'm scared to death, because of the influence my name and words might have. I thought all I wanted to do was sing."

Despite fame and fortune and the changes they have brought, Johnny Cash is still tied to his past in many ways. He is frequently seen in blue coveralls hoeing his garden — intent upon an activity tied to the soil to work off tension and restlessness. The woods in which he lives are on the banks of the Cumberland River where an ancient Cherokee tribe once lived. And the house, though costly, has the rustic touches of a sod roof and square-hewn logs from pioneer barns.

The Cashes' home life, too, has many traditional features. June gets up at 5:30 a.m. to bake bread and prepare a family breakfast. She cuts Johnny's hair, irons his trousers, and often prepares squirrels that he has shot for dinner. His favorite meal is an old one — runner beans and turnip greens cooked with bacon. He also likes

fried ham with red-eye gravy, made by adding

strong black coffee to ham grease. "No flour," Johnny says. "If it's got flour it's called slingshot gravy."

And reminiscent of his family's old "Daddy Sang Bass" days on the farm are "musicales" — events held three times a year in the Cashes' living room. Each guest must perform as the guitar is passed around. Bob Dylan introduced "Lay Lady Lay" at one of these sessions, and Judy Collins first sang "Both Sides Now."

The most powerful force in Cash's current life is religion. This recent emphasis may also have roots in the traditions of his youth, when he attended Baptist and Pentecostal churches and sang hymns with his family. What has happened to bring about this change in the life of a person who once described himself as "mean as hell?"

On May 9, 1971, Johnny Cash attended a small Pentecostal church outside of Nashville. According to witnesses, when the preacher made his altar call to the congregation, Johnny walked down the aisle, kneeled at the alter and dedicated his life to Jesus Christ. He said later, "I don't have a career anymore. What I have now is a ministry . . . I've lived all my life for the devil up 'til now, and from here on I'm going to live it for the Lord."

Since Cash's conversion, his career has taken a new direction. The nature of his performances has changed. The Evangel Temple choir has

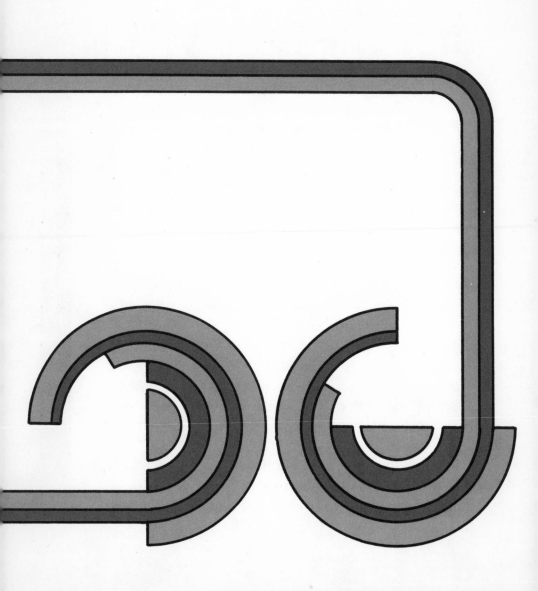

frequently appeared with him on stage and in 1972 provided the choral background for his Columbia recording of "A Thing Called Love." Cash also appeared at the Jesus Music Festival, "Explo '72," with Billy Graham; the audience numbered almost 200,000 people. In a Las Vegas show, he included a segment on religion that involved singing Christian songs while pictures of Jesus were projected onto the wall. This public testimony received both compliments and criticism, but he intends to continue such features in his performances.

In 1972, Johnny Cash embarked on a project that he calls the proudest work of his career. He made his own documentary film on the life of Christ. It includes country music composed by Cash and such people as John Denver, Kris Kristofferson, and Larry Gatlin. The cast of **Gospel Road,** which was filmed in Israel, includes June Carter Cash as Mary Magdalene and Johnny's sister Reba as the Virgin Mary.

Johnny Cash expects this new dimension to expand his contributions to society. He says emphatically, "I want to go on singin' forever. Maybe I'll be out there, 65 years old, and they'll be sayin', 'Get off that stage, you old bum.' But I mean to be out there."

However long he performs, Johnny Cash will remain a complex, unpredictable legend in country music.